Graceful Beginnings

Short and Easy for Anyone New to the Bible

The Walk from
FEAR TO FAITH

Trusting God with Your Fears
(Study 6 Old Testament Women Who Did)

MELANIE NEWTON

JOYFUL
WALK
BIBLE
STUDIES

The Walk from Fear to Faith: Trusting God with Your Fears (Study 6 Old Testament Women Who Did)

© 2025 by Melanie Newton. All rights reserved.

Published by Joyful Walk Press. Flower Mound, TX.

ISBN: 979-8-9925750-4-0

For questions about the use of this study guide or for bulk orders, please email us at melanienewton.com.

Cover photo acquired from best-wallpaper.net, "Summer-morning-nature-forest-trail-sun-light-rays.jpg," a public domain image.

Melanie Newton is the author of "Graceful Beginnings" books for anyone new to the Bible and "Joyful Walk Bible Studies" for established Christians. Her mission is to help women learn to study the Bible for themselves and to grow their Bible-teaching skills to lead others.

Joyful Walk Bible Studies are grace-based studies for women of all ages. Each study guide follows the inductive method of Bible study (observation, interpretation, application) in a warm and inviting format. We pray that you will find *The Walk from Fear to Faith* to be a resource that God will use to strengthen you in your faith walk with Him.

Christ-Focused • Grace-Based • Bible-Rich

JOYFUL WALK PRESS
Flower Mound, TX

MELANIE NEWTON

Melanie Newton is a Louisiana girl who made the choice to follow Jesus while attending LSU. She and her husband Ron married and moved to Texas for him to attend Dallas Theological Seminary. They stayed in Texas where Ron led a wilderness camping ministry for troubled youth for many years. Ron now helps corporations with their challenging employees and is the author of the top-rated business book, *No Jerks on the Job*.

Melanie jumped into raising three Texas-born children and serving in ministry to women at her church. Through the years, the Lord has given her opportunity to do Bible teaching and to write grace-based Bible studies for women that are now available from her website (melanienewton.com) and on Bible.org. *Graceful Beginnings* books are for anyone new to the Bible. *Joyful Walk Bible Studies* are for maturing Christians.

Melanie Newton loves to help women learn how to study the Bible for themselves. She also teaches online courses for women to grow their Bible-teaching skills to help others—all with the goal of getting to know Jesus more along the way. Her heart's desire is to encourage you to have a joyful relationship with Jesus Christ so you are willing to share that experience with others around you.

Jesus took hold of me in 1972, and I have been on this great adventure ever since. My life is a gift of God, full of blessings in the midst of difficult challenges. The more I have learned and experienced God's absolutely amazing grace, the more I have discovered my faith walk to be a joyful one. I am still seeking that joyful walk every day.

Melanie

OTHER BIBLE STUDIES BY MELANIE NEWTON

Graceful Beginnings Series books for anyone new to the Bible:

A Fresh Start (basics for new Christians)
Painting the Portrait of Jesus (the Gospel of John)
The God You Can Know (the character of God)
Grace Overflowing (an overview of Paul's 13 letters)
The Walk from Fear to Faith (7 Old Testament women)
Satisfied by His Love (women who knew Jesus)
Seek the Treasure (study of Ephesians)
Pathways to a Joyful Walk (6 pathways to a life filled with joy)

Joyful Walk Bible Studies for growing Christians:

Adorn Yourself with Godliness (1 Timothy and Titus, also +Spanish)
Everyday Women, Ever Faithful God (Old Testament women, +Spanish)
Connecting Faith to Life on Planet Earth (Genesis 1-11; Revelation)
Graceful Living (the essentials for a grace-based Christian life)
Graceful Living Today (a devotional journal for a joyful life)
Healthy Living (Colossians and Philemon)
Heartbreak to Hope (the Gospel of Mark)
Identity: Sticking to Your Faith in a Pull-Apart World (Ezra - Malachi)
Knowing Jesus, Knowing Joy (Philippians, +Spanish)
Live Out His Love (New Testament women)
Perspective (1and 2 Thessalonians)
Profiles of Perseverance (Old Testament men, also +Spanish)
Radical Acts (Acts)
Reboot, Renew, Rejoice (1 and 2 Chronicles)
The God-Dependent Woman (2 Corinthians)
To Be Found Faithful (2 Timothy)

Resources for leading others

Be a Christ-Focused Small Group Leader
Leap into Lifestyle Disciplemaking
Bible Study Leadership Made Easy (online video course)
Painting the Picture of Jesus (the "I Am's" of Jesus lessons)
Teaching Children the God They Can Know (the character of God)
Download our catalogue and get resources for your spiritual growth at melanienewton.com.

Contents

Contents

Introduction

GRACEFUL BEGINNINGS

The *Graceful Beginnings* books are Bible studies specifically designed for anyone new to the Bible—whether you are a new Christian or you just feel insecure about understanding the Bible. The short and easy lessons will introduce you to your God and His way of approaching life in simple terms that can be easily understood.

Just as a newborn baby needs to know the love and trustworthiness of her parents, the new Christian needs to know and experience the love and trustworthiness of her God. *A Fresh Start* is the first book in the series, laying a good foundation of truth for you to grasp and apply to your life. The other books in the series can be done in any order.

SOME BIBLE BASICS

Throughout these lessons, you will use a Bible to answer questions as you discover treasure about your life with Christ. The Bible is one book containing a collection of 66 books combined together for our benefit. It is divided into two main parts: the Old Testament and the New Testament.

The Old Testament tells the story of the beginning of the world and God's promises to mankind given through the nation of Israel. It tells how the people of Israel obeyed and disobeyed God over many, many years. All the stories and messages in the Old Testament lead up to Jesus Christ's coming to the earth.

The New Testament tells the story of Jesus Christ, the early Christians, and God's promises to all those who believe in Jesus. You can think of the Old Testament as "before Christ" and the New Testament as "after Christ."

Each book of the Bible is divided into chapters and verses within those chapters to make it easier to study. Bible references include the book name, chapter number and verse number(s). For example, Ephesians 2:8 refers to the New Testament book of Ephesians, the 2nd chapter, and verse 8 within that 2nd chapter. Printed Bibles have a "Table of Contents" in the front to help you locate books by page number. Bible apps also have a contents list by book and chapter.

The Bible verses highlighted at the beginning of each lesson in this study are from the New International Version® (NIV®) unless otherwise indicated. You can use any version of the Bible to answer the questions, but using a more easy-to-read translation (NIRV, NLT, NET, ESV) will help you gain confidence in understanding what you are reading. You can find all these translations in "the Bible App" or on biblegateway.com.

This study capitalizes certain pronouns referring to God, Jesus and the Holy Spirit—He, Him, His, Himself—just to make the reading of the study information less confusing. Some Bible translations likewise capitalize those pronouns referring to God; others do not. It is simply a matter of preference, not a requirement.

OLD TESTAMENT SUMMARY

About 1700 years after God created everything, He sent judgment on a rebellious race through a worldwide Flood. He later separated the nations with different languages and scattered them from Babel. Abraham, Isaac, and Jacob were founding fathers of the Hebrew people. Sold into slavery, Joseph became a powerful foreign leader. The Israelites developed into a great nation for ~400 years in Egypt, until their deliverance from bondage. Then Moses took the people across the Red Sea and taught them God's Law at Mt. Sinai. Joshua led the Israelites into the Promised Land after a 40-year trek in the wilderness because of unbelief.

During the transition toward monarchy, there were deliverer-rulers called "Judges," the last of whom was Samuel. The first three Hebrew kings—Saul, David, and Solomon—each ruled 40 years. Under Rehoboam, the Hebrew nation divided into northern and southern kingdoms, respectively called Israel and Judah. Prophets warned against worshipping the foreign god Baal. After the reign of 19 wicked kings in the north, Assyria conquered and scattered the northern kingdom. In the south, 20 kings ruled for ~350 years, until Babylon took the people into captivity for 70 years. Zerubbabel, Ezra, and Nehemiah led the Jews back into Jerusalem over a 100-year period. More than 400 "silent years" spanned the gap between Malachi and Matthew.

The 39 books in the Old Testament are divided into 4 main categories:

- "THE LAW" (5 books)—the beginning of the nation of Israel as God's chosen people; God giving His Laws to the people that made them distinct from the rest of the nations.

- "HISTORY" (12 books)—narratives that reveal what happened from the time the people entered the Promised Land right after Moses died until 400 years before Christ was born.

- "POETRY & WISDOM" (5 books)—take place at the same time as the history books but are set apart because they are written as poems and have a lot of wise teaching in them.

- "PROPHETS" (17 books)—concurrent with the books of history and, except for Lamentations, reflect the name of the prophet through whom God spoke to the nation of Israel.

ELEMENTS OF EACH LESSON

This book covers the lives of several Old Testament women. Each lesson begins with a brief history of a particular Old Testament time period and then covers the lives of 1-2 women who lived then. The lessons are arranged chronologically following the simple Old Testament timeline below.

Historical Period	Years BC	Woman Studied
The Patriarchs	2100 - 1800	Sarah
Israel in Egypt / the Exodus	1800 - 1450	Jochebed, Miriam
Conquest of the Land	1450 - 1400	Rahab
Kingdom	850 - 800	Zarephath Widow Prophet's Widow Shunammite Woman

To help us consider those women to be real women, I suggest names in the lessons for those who are nameless. You will see 'quotes' around the suggested name. ☺

1. Each lesson begins with a Bible verse that relates to the focus of the lesson and a prayer. Prayer is just talking to God as conversation with someone who loves you dearly. The beginning prayer simply asks Jesus to teach you through the lesson.

2. This is followed by a description of the time period and a simple study of the passages that tell each woman's story. Read the Bible verses and answer the associated questions. This study uses the NIV translation. We recommend you use that or other easy-to-read translations (CSB, NLT, NET, ESV). See "Bible Basics" above for online sources of these.

3. "THE WALK FROM FEAR TO FAITH" section at the end of the study questions, asks you to consider how each Old Testament woman overcame her fear so you can do the same. We then encourage you to "JOURNAL YOUR FAITH STORY," writing something that relates to what you learned in the lesson. Your faith story is your biography of God's faithfulness to you and your response back to Him.

4. A short teaching section ("FAITH IN ACTION") follows each lesson and gives you help in taking action so you can walk from fear to faith. You can listen to each of these as a podcast from melanienewton.com/podcasts. Look for "1: OT Women" to find the one for each lesson. You can also find these podcasts on most podcast providers. Or you can read the blogs associated with the podcasts at melanienewton.com/blog. Choose OT Women category then scroll to find the title you want. Listen to the first podcast as an introduction to the study.

5. Every "FAITH IN ACTION" section is followed by a "REFLECT" time for you to respond to what you learned and some prayer prompts related to the lesson.

SMALL GROUP DISCUSSION GUIDELINES

While you can work through these lessons as a personal study, this topic is perfect to use for small groups. Share the following suggested guidelines with the group members to maximize your discussion group experience.

➢ Set aside some time each week to do the study questions so that you will get to know God better.

➢ Consistently attend whether your lesson is done or not. You will learn from the discussion.

➢ Respect each other's insights. Listen thoughtfully. Share your own insights, but do not dominate the discussion.

➢ Avoid trying to fix each other's challenges but lean on Jesus instead.

➢ Celebrate unity in Christ by avoiding controversial subjects such as politics, divisive issues and denominational differences.

➢ Maintain confidentiality of whatever is shared within the group.

Enjoy your small group discussion and learn from one another. As you journal parts of your story and share that with your group members, you will have a greater connection with each other. And you will have more reason to praise our ever-faithful God as you see and hear how He has been faithful to each of you through the years. A small group is a great place to share your "Walk from Fear to Faith." Discussing the lesson and the teaching session should take about an hour, making this an easy study to fit into a busy workday schedule.

Suggested Leader Guide for Group Discussion:

You can download a more detailed discussion guide at melanienewton.com/ fear-to-faith. Or follow the suggestions below:

1. Pray for the Holy Spirit to teach you what He wants you to know through the lesson.

2. Work through the lesson together, reading the Bible verses and discussing the questions. Predetermine which of the explanatory paragraphs you will read as a group.

3. Discuss THE WALK FROM FEAR TO FAITH questions, read the summary paragraph and say the four truths together.

4. Share your response to the JOURNAL YOUR FAITH WALK section.

5. Discuss parts of the FAITH-IN-ACTION section that you want to emphasize. REFLECT on the teaching.

6. Pray for the group members – about their fears and decisions to trust God in them. Thank God for His grace and His love for you.

7. Remind each person to do the next lesson and listen to the related podcast before the group meets again.

Enjoy!

The Walk from Fear to Faith

Jill Briscoe once said, "Women are a fear-driven, performance-oriented species." She is right. Fear is an ever-present emotion with us. Real fears and imagined fears. Is it realistic to think we can live without fear? No!

Fear is a normal human emotion designed by God to alert us to danger so that we will take action against it. Yet, fear can take root in us and cause us to give way to panic and hysteria. God knows this about us. I am so grateful for that! I can remember times in my life when something happened suddenly that caused that creepy-crawly feeling down my back. A car cutting in front of me sending me to change lanes quickly, hoping there was not an 18-wheeler occupying that lane. One night, a feeling of fear for my oldest daughter's safety hit me in the chest. I quickly prayed for her protection. Of course, she did not answer her phone when I called so I had to wait until the next morning to hear from her that she was okay. What. A. Scary. Night.

Thankfully, some wise mentors have taught me to trust God all the time, especially when I am afraid. One such wise woman, Vickie Kraft, drilled a couple of verses into my heart and mind.

> When I am afraid, I will trust in you. In God, whose word I praise, in God I trust; I will not be afraid. What can mortal man do to me? (Psalm 56:3-4)

This wise friend said, "Melanie, the psalmist doesn't say, '**If** I am afraid.' He says, '**When** I am afraid.' When we are afraid, God wants us to trust Him and not give way to fear."

If fear alerts us to danger so we will take action against it, the most significant action is to not give in to fear but to trust God instead. That is the walk from fear to faith. And we can experience God's faithfulness through any trouble, danger, suffering, or pain that we face. God is faithful always.

In His faithfulness, our God does not leave us guessing as to what this walk from fear to faith looks like. In His enduring, living Word, He has recorded examples for us to follow—women of the past who put their hope in God, did what was right, and did not give way to fear (1 Peter 3:5-6). The writer of Hebrews 11 gave us specific examples who chose to live by faith in the midst of terrifying circumstances.

So in this study, we are going to look at their lives—these Old Testament women who learned to trust in God's faithfulness and goodness. They were ordinary females with the same emotions and tendencies to panic that we have. Each one of these women had a story, and that story has been shared over and over and over to millions of eager listeners. You might be surprised how many times the scriptures refer to them actually telling their story in one form or another. You are going to get to know it as you get to know them. It is a connection with real women. As we study their lives, we will see an ever-faithful God in action, a faithful God whose character never changes.

God is as faithful now in our everyday circumstances of life as He was years ago to them. We can feel confidence in His presence and active involvement, even when we cannot see it. And knowing this, we can trust in Him whenever we are afraid. Trust is faith. Faith is confidence in God—His existence, His character, and His faithfulness to those who place themselves in His care.

That is the "Walk from Fear to Faith"—learning to trust God whenever we are afraid.

As we join these Old Testament women moving from fear to faith, we will see consistent truths that we can apply to our lives today in our faith walk. In every case, we know that God loved her. He knew what was going on in her life. He was able to do something about it. During her faith walk, a loving God said "no" to some things. Yet, she chose to trust Him rather than submit to fear. And God rewarded her faith with an outpouring of His blessing in other ways.

Likewise, God may not choose to rescue you from everything that is threatening you. But in any and all situations, you can count on these truths…

    #1 God loves me.
    #2 God knows what is going on in my life.
    #3 God can do something about it.
    #4 I can trust His goodness in whatever He chooses to do!

Count on these truths and live each day believing they are true. It is going to be a great journey. And I am so glad to be walking beside you!

Melanie Newton

1 Got Fear? Trust Your God

Recommended: *Listen to the podcast "Old Testament Women Walk from Fear to Faith."*

When I am afraid, I put my trust in you. In God, whose word I praise—in God I trust and am not afraid. What can mere man do to me? PSALM 56:3-4

> Pray: Lord Jesus, please teach me through this lesson.

THE GIFT OF FEAR

You know that feeling. The pit in your stomach, pounding of your heart, and rush of your thoughts as you go from just the possibility of a job loss to starving and being homeless on the streets—all in a matter of seconds. Gripped by fear, although an imagined one.

Fear is a normal human emotion designed by God to alert us to danger so that we will take action against it. It has a purpose. It tells us to take precautions, to be wise in our dealings with strangers and strange situations. We need to think of it as a gift. God gave it to us before sin happened (Genesis 2:16-17) and used it throughout the Bible to warn people of the consequences of disobeying Him.

We know fear has a dark side as well. Bible teacher Jill Briscoe declared this, "Women are a fear-driven, performance-oriented species." Just watching the daily news can panic us. But what did she mean by fear-driven? Why would fear drive us? And what does fear drive us to do?

Women in general are created with a nesting instinct, a need for security and stability, and a desire to control our environment in order to create that security for us and for those we love. Our American way of thinking is this: we can fix it—whatever "IT" is. When we cannot fix it, we panic.

Fear can be real or imagined. For me, a real fear is meeting a snake in my woodsy yard while gardening. I know they are there so I carefully do everything I can to avoid interaction with them. I experienced an imagined fear as my youngest daughter was growing up. That fear manifested itself in ongoing nightmares about her being kidnapped or molested. She was never threatened that way, but she was friendly and outgoing. I guess I thought she was more vulnerable than my older, more cautious daughter. When that young daughter became a strong teen girl who was daily hockey-checking her older brother into the wall as they met each other in the hallway, those nightmares stopped. I guess my subconscious recognized that she could handle herself.

Consider examples of both real fears and imagined ones in your life.

Fear is an ever-present emotion with most women—real fears as well as imagined ones. Is it realistic to think we can live without fear? No!

Our faithful God understands this about us.

Read Psalm 56:3-4.

Write out these verses in the space provided below.

Reading back over the verses, underline the phrases that tell you what to do when you are afraid.

Notice that David did not write, "**If** I am afraid." He said, "**When** I am afraid." Fear will happen.

God gave us the emotion of fear. It was given with a purpose—*to alert us to danger so that we will take action against it.* Yet, sudden fear can cause us to be terrified. We can let fear take root in us so that we give way to panic and hysteria. Does that ring any bells with you? Are you prone to hysterics?

God knows this about us. When we are afraid, God wants us to trust Him and not give way to fear. Learning to do that is our **walk from fear to faith**.

TRUSTING A FAITHFUL GOD

> When we look at life just with our own eyes, we become fearful, pessimistic, & negative. We become people who feel, 'I don't know if that can work. I don't know if I can get through this.' When we look at the Scriptures and begin to...see how God empowered normal average people like you and I, the Holy Spirit takes the Word of God and strengthens us and gives us courage that we did not know we had. (Steve Hixon, pastor)

Because God understands this tendency to fear and panic, the Holy Spirit inspired Peter to write to us women in 1 Peter 3:3-6 words that strengthen us and give us courage we did not know we could have.

Read 1 Peter 3:3-6.

What does God consider to be of great worth in His sight (verse 4)?

Although the focus of this passage is a marriage relationship, the principles relate to any woman's character ("inner self"), especially the qualities of a GENTLE and QUIET spirit that are of great worth in God's sight—valuable, precious. These enable a woman to "do what is right and not give way to fear" (verse 6).

But you may be thinking, "How can that apply to me? I have a bubbly personality. I am not naturally quiet." Before you start feeling irritated about these words or afraid that you could never measure up to this, let us find out what "gentle" and "quiet" actually mean.

Gentle = Controlled strength

"GENTLE" does not mean passive, weak, or someone who cannot help herself. Rather, it means **"controlled strength."** Picture a mother cradling a newborn. She has the physical strength to harm that child but does not because her strength is under control. If you are going to have a gentle spirit, what will you need? Strength under control.

A woman with a gentle spirit has a humble heart that bows itself before God, recognizes God's dealings with her as good, and chooses not to be contentious or resistant against Him. That is strength under control.

Quiet = Tranquility from within

"QUIET" does not mean whisper, silent, or bland. It does mean **"tranquility arising from within"** and includes the idea of causing no disturbance to others. Think how a woman's hysterics affect those around her—family, friends, and coworkers.

A woman with a quiet spirit has an inner peace and calmness in the midst of any circumstance. Have you experienced that kind of peace?

Gentleness and peace are the fruit of the Holy Spirit's work (Gal. 5: 22-23) in a believer's life and available to every Christian woman who desires them—that includes you and me! We can have a tranquil spirit in the midst of chaos. See how it fits with the "strength under control" mindset?

> *Why do you think these qualities in a woman would be of great worth to God?*

> *Now that you know the real meanings of these words, are you more likely to desire these qualities? Why?*

Read these verses again.

> *For this is the way the holy women of the past who (1) put their*
> *hope in God...used to make themselves beautiful...like*
> *Sarah...You are her daughters if you (2) do what is right and*
> *(3) do not give way to fear. (1 Peter 3:5-6, NIV)*

In the verses written above, underline the three choices
women can make—identified by (1), (2), and (3).

Peter identified these examples for us as "holy women of the past." The word "holy" means set apart for God's special use. These women are holy because they had learned to trust in God when they were afraid. As holy women, these women were beautiful in God's eyes (regardless of their outward appearance, age, or social status). This beauty attributed to them by God Himself was based on three choices they made ("used to make themselves beautiful") that every woman can also make:

➢ Choice #1: **You can put your hope in God**—in God and His Word rather than the unreliability of ourselves or others.

➢ Choice #2: **You can do what is right**—according to God's way of approaching life, not the world's way, especially those cultural practices that go against God's Word.

➢ Choice #3: **You can choose to not give way to fear.** Let us examine this one more closely.

Choose to not give way to fear

Choose to not give way to fear. What does that mean?

We know this: God is not saying, "Don't ever feel fear." God gave us the gift of fear as **a normal human emotion designed to alert us to danger so we can take action against it**. He is saying, "Here is why you don't have to be terrified and paralyzed by your fear." We are to face our troubles without panic and hysteria. We are to TRUST GOD—in whom we have put our hope and by whose Word we are taught to do what is right.

Underline the definition for fear in the above paragraph.

Have you ever felt terrified? How did you respond?

God says that having a gentle and quiet inner spirit will make it easier for us to not get so terrified and stay that way.

What is harder for God: rescuing us from desperate circumstances or developing in us a gentle and quiet spirit?

Why?

Did you select the "developing in us a gentle and quiet spirit?" I agree because it involves our cooperation! Is it too difficult for Him? No! A humble, peaceful heart makes it easier for us to face troubles without panic and hysteria and to choose to trust in the faithfulness of God.

We have a faithful God. That is not imaginary. In 1 Peter 3, Sarah represents several other everyday women who lived in Old Testament days who put their hope in God and found Him worthy of their trust. This was their walk from fear to faith. What is that?

Choosing Faith

In the Bible, "walk" refers to following a certain course of life or conducting oneself in a certain way. It is how you choose to live daily, what motivates you, what guides you, and what decisions you make in how you respond to life. Will your daily walk follow God's way of approaching life or the world's way? Your walk is your choice.

For the purposes of this study, your choice involves moving away from fear and toward faith. Most of us have a pretty good understanding of fear in our lives. But what is faith? God describes what faith looks like through the writer of Hebrews.

Read Hebrews 11:1.

How is faith described?

Read Hebrews 11:6.

What must one believe about God?

Did you notice that faith is related to confidence? Confident hope and confident assurance is based on what you believe is true. That confidence is in the facts that our God exists and is good to anyone who seeks Him. This confidence pleases Him. Hebrews 11 gives examples of men and women who had this confidence in God. They were commended by God for their faith (verse 2).

Read the following verses. In each, who chose faith in God over giving way to fear?

- Hebrews 11:11—

- Hebrews 11:23—

- Hebrews 11:31—

Read Hebrews 11:35 (first half of verse).

By faith, what did these women receive?

These are the women who are our examples of choosing faith in God over giving way to fear. Old Testament women.

CONNECTING WITH OLD TESTAMENT WOMEN

You may have very little knowledge of the Old Testament so these women may be strangers to you. Even though these women lived years ago, they were still women like we are.

As everyday women, they cooked meals, did laundry, and raised children. They had responsibilities inside and outside of their homes, including home businesses. They experienced hormone fluctuations and menopause. They laughed with their friends, differed with their mates, and cried when a loved one died. They wrote songs and played musical instruments. I bet they all found ways to use their 20,000 words per day!

At one time, they were 20-somethings, then 40-somethings, then 60-somethings and maybe more. They wore beads, earrings, and ankle bracelets. Their hair needed to be combed and fixed, and it turned grey as they aged. No doubt, some of them, if not all, had something on their bodies that sagged!

These women also experienced fear at various times in their lives just like we do. They faced invading enemies, sick family members, and empty pantries. They faced creditors and surprise houseguests. They even had "bad" days when things did not go right, sometimes due to their own choices.

These were **EVERYDAY WOMEN**, just like we are.

As women in general, what kind of life experiences for them might have been the same as your own life experiences?

What kinds of fears did these women face that you may also face?

Their stories—snippets of their biographies—are preserved for us to get to know them and to know their God who is also our God—an **EVER-FAITHFUL** God whose character never changes.

They knew Him by the personal name *Yahweh* (YAH-weh). In our English translations, it is usually written as LORD in capital letters. In the Old Testament, you will find the phrase "the LORD your God" or "the LORD our God" at least 500 times. Every time, that phrase is emphasizing, "We have a personal God. His name is *Yahweh*." It is the name by which God wished to be known and worshiped in Israel and by Israel, and it means, "I am." This name expressed His character as **constant, dependable, and faithful**.

Jesus applied God's name "I am" to Himself (John 4:26; 8:59), thus declaring Himself to be God. The ever faithful, promise-keeping God of the Old Testament is embodied in the Lord Jesus Christ of the New Testament and forever. We still have a personal God.

THE WALK FROM FEAR TO FAITH

Read John 14:27.

What does Jesus promise to you?

Read John 16:33.

What does Jesus promise to you?

What might be holding you back from trusting Him whenever you are afraid?

He is with you through any trouble. You can trust Him. Our God is trustworthy!

> When we experience anxiety or fear, the enemy can try to use it as an opportunity to make us feel guilt or shame. That is when we pause and ask God for help, knowing He understands and never condemns us. (Holley Gerth, "Fear Not," *Homelife Magazine,* March 2016)

JOURNAL YOUR FAITH STORY

Describe a problem in your life (current or past) where you needed to make a choice to do the right thing, but you were afraid of the consequences resulting from that choice. What have you learned about trusting God and living by faith in that area?

"EMBRACE 4 TRUTHS ESSENTIAL TO FAITH"

Recommended: *Listen to the podcast "The Walk from Fear to Faith-4 Essential Truths." Use the section below as a listener guide.*

When we look at life just with our own eyes, we become fearful, pessimistic, & negative. We think to ourselves, "Nothing's going to work. I don't know if I can get through this." But when we look at the Bible and begin to see how God has empowered everyday people like you and I, the Holy Spirit takes the Word of God to strengthen us and give us courage that we did not know we had. Our examples are Old Testament women. As we join these Old Testament women on their faith walk, we will see consistent truths that we can embrace and apply to our lives today in our WALK FROM FEAR TO FAITH.

Truth #1: God loves you

John 3:16; John 16:27; Romans 5:5; Eph. 5:1; Col. 3:12

You are part of that world that God loves. And as a believer in Jesus, God the Father loves you and pours out His love into your heart so you can experience His love.

Truth #2: God knows what is going on in your life

Matthew 6:31-32; Psalm 139:1-10

God is everywhere and knows everything. So God knows what is going on in your life. He knows your needs and how best to meet them.

Truth #3: God can do something about it

Genesis 18:14; Luke 1:37

Is anything impossible for the Lord? The answer is, NO! Our God is all-powerful. He is capable of doing anything He chooses to do that is in agreement with His character and His purposes.

Truth #4: You can trust His goodness in whatever He chooses to do

Psalm 119:68; Proverbs 3:5

The Bible says that God is good, and what He does is good. It is a choice to trust God and bank on His goodness.

As we study each of these women—our mentors, we will see that during her faith walk, a loving God said "no" to some things. Yet, she chose to trust Him rather than submit to fear. And God rewarded her faith with an outpouring of His blessing in other ways. You and I can do the same.

Dear friends, God may not choose to rescue you from everything that is threatening you. But in any and all situations, you can embrace these truths, making them personal...

#1. God loves me
#2. God knows what is going on in my life
#3. God can do something about it
#4. I can trust His goodness in whatever He chooses to do

You can count on that!

> When You don't move the mountains I'm needing You to move
> When You don't part the waters I wish I could walk through
> When You don't give the answers as I cry out to You
> I will trust, I will trust, I will trust in You!
> (Lauren Daigle, "Trust in You")

REFLECT

What is causing you fear today? What are your choices for acting on that fear? Apply the 4 truths to your situation.

Pray about your fears and decisions you are making to trust God in them. Thank God for His grace toward you and His love for you.

2 God Is Bigger than Your Weaknesses

BY FAITH...SARAH

*For this is the way the holy women of the past who put their hope in God used to adorn themselves....like Sarah...**You are her daughters if you do what is right and do not give way to fear.*** 1 PETER 3:5-6

> Pray: Lord Jesus, please teach me through this lesson.

A little bit of history

Sarah lived during the biblical time of "The Patriarchs" (2100-1800 BC). The term patriarch denotes the father or male leader of a family or tribe. In the Bible, "patriarchs" usually refer to the three main characters whose lives are documented in Genesis 12-50—Abraham, Isaac, and Jacob.

During Sarah's life, the great civilizations of Egypt and Mesopotamia dominated the Ancient Near East. Archeologists have discovered that Ur (in today's Iraq) was a thriving city of Mesopotamia with efficient government, impressive buildings, and lots of amenities (like flush toilets). Yet, it was also characterized by idol worship.

Under God's direction, Abraham willingly left Ur, with its culture and conveniences, for the land of Canaan (today's Israel). Patriarchal life was semi-nomadic as they wandered from place to place, searching for grazing land and water for their animals. Wealth was measured in animal herds and movable goods such as silver, gold, and tents.

The patriarchal era is important to us. Through the descendants of Abraham and his wife Sarah, God began to develop a people of His own. The Abrahamic Covenant (God's unconditional pledge to Abraham) contains many precious promises including numerous offspring, dedicated land, and a plan to bless all people of the earth. These promises passed on to Isaac and Jacob (known as "Israel," a name God gave him). Jacob's sons formed the nucleus of the twelve tribes of Israel the nation. Through one son's kindness (Joseph), the rest of Israel (72 people) entered Egypt and grew into a mighty nation.

Sarah is mentioned more times in Scripture than any other woman, even Mary the mother of Jesus. She is the matriarch of the Jews and the first woman mentioned in Hebrews 11, what is often called "The Faith Hall of Fame."

Though she lived 4000 years ago, God uses Sarah as an example for us to follow in 1 Peter 3:3-6. We should, therefore, want to find out about Sarah. *Who was she? How was she like us? How can we be like her?* Let us join her journey.

Moving from home (Sarah is ~65 years old)

Although they are called Abram and Sarai in the early passages, for consistency's sake, we will use the more common "Abraham" and "Sarah" (names later given to them by God). Genesis 17:17 tells us she is ten years younger than Abraham.

Read Genesis 11:29-12:5.

Describe Sarah and her circumstances in life at this time.

Barrenness for a woman in Sarah's time was very painful, like it is for a woman in our time. Sons especially were needed to carry on the family name and livelihood. When Sarah left Haran, moving to who-knows-where, she was willing to cooperate with God's plan for Abraham even when it was tough for her.

How are you at encouraging your friend or spouse to follow God's leading, even if it changes your life?

Read Genesis 12:10-20.

Abraham's "Tell them you are my sister" plan, though making no sense to us, seemed to have merit in his time. One historian said that if a married man of Abraham's day found himself in enemy territory, he could be killed for his wife. But if Abraham were known as her brother, someone wanting her would have to make marriage arrangements with Abraham because in that society, a woman's brother gave his sister in marriage. Thus, Abraham would have been the negotiator, supposedly giving him the chance to act in his own interest. Sarah was his half-sister from another mother (Genesis 20:12).

Sarah went along with Abraham's "Tell them you are my sister" plan because she was willing to do what he thought was needed to preserve his life. Remember that as the Holy Spirit inspired Peter to write his letter, God honored Sarah for not giving way to fear (1 Peter 3:5-6).

How is Sarah described (verses 11, 14)?

Sarah found herself in what situation (verse 15)?

What might have been Sarah's emotions during this time?

When Abraham failed to protect Sarah in this incident, what did God do for her?

11 years later (Sarah is ~76)

In ancient times, a man who had no son could adopt a favored servant as heir to his possessions (Genesis 15:1-6). Or a man who had no son could take a second wife to produce an heir. Some marriage contracts even spelled out this provision. A wife was obligated to have children. We would consider that "Plan A." If she could not, she was required to let her husband take another wife who could (Plan B). Abraham, however, had not already sought a second wife.

Read Genesis 16:1-6.

What was Sarah's "Plan B" to fix Abraham's need for an heir (verses 2-3)?

This was an accepted cultural practice of her time for a childless wife to provide another "womb" for an heir. But Sarah's "Plan B" becomes a nightmare (verse 4)! Our example was no perfect woman. She was just like we are. Look at her behavior!

How did Sarah react to Hagar's pregnancy (verses 5-6)?

What was threatened in Sarah's life, and what confirmation do you think she needed from her husband?

13 years later (Sarah is 89)

God once again told Abraham His plan to provide descendants for Abraham and a faithful people for Himself (Gen. 17:1-2).

Read Genesis 17:15-19.

How does God's plan include Sarah (verses 15-16)?

Read Genesis 18:1-15.

When the visitors came by Abraham's tent (one of whom was the Lord), where was Sarah (verses 6-9)?

What did the Lord give Sarah for the first time (verse 10)?

What was Sarah's initial response and why (verses 11-12)?

The Hebrew word translated "pleasure" in verse 12 is "eden," a term synonymous with sensual pleasure. By the way, Abraham also laughed (Genesis 17:17). Does it surprise you that Sarah might have given up hope of ever having a baby?

What confirmation did God give to her (verse 14)?

God's plan is completely different from what you could ever imagine and much more glorious than you would ever expect. (Mike Messerli)

Have you noticed this in your life? Is anything really too hard for the Lord?

When the Lord confronted her about laughing (verse 13), what did Sarah do (verse 15)?

What was the Lord's response (verse 15)? Do you think He knew her pretty well by now?

Shortly after the "tent" visit. Abraham nearly jeopardized the whole situation by again placing Sarah in another man's harem (Genesis 20). He fails in the same area of faith in which he failed 25 years earlier. At 90 years of age, she was taken into a harem of the reigning king. This gives further information regarding Sarah's beauty. God must have turned on her hormones again in a big way—super estrogen!!

1 year later (Sarah is 90)

Read Genesis 21:1-7.

What is declared about God in verse 1?

What did He do for Sarah (verse 2)?

What story did she have to tell (verses 6 and 7)?

The name Isaac means "he laughs." In what ways is Isaac an appropriate name for this baby?

Through this whole experience, how do we know that God loved Sarah as much as Abraham?

When she got pregnant, can you imagine the hope building in her heart? I think she was smiling and giggling to herself all nine months. Then, Isaac is born. His name reminds her of their laughter. Is it possible that God delighted in making these two old people laugh?

3 years later (Sarah is now ~93)

Read Genesis 21:8-13.

What problem did Sarah recognize between Ishmael and Isaac (verse 9)?

What was Sarah's solution (verse 10)?

How did Abraham respond (verse 11)?

What was God's solution (verse 12)?

Every wife loves that God told Abraham to listen to his wife! God faithfully took care of Hagar and Ishmael, too (verses 14-20).

I am so glad God gave us Sarah for an example—a beauty queen whose life was rarely smooth or easy. She went childless for many years. Her husband's fears put her at risk by his decisions. And she made a huge mistake that made life miserable for her. She was an everyday woman like you and I are. We can relate to some things about her life. It is harder to relate to someone who did everything right. Sarah is one example to follow in believing that **God is worthy of our trust**.

THE WALK FROM FEAR TO FAITH

What situations in Sarah's life could have "terrified" her?

Considering those "opportunities" for being terrified, in which ones did Sarah, by faith, do what was right and not give way to fear?

God loved Sarah. He knew what was going on in her life. He was able to do something about it. But God did not give Sarah a child early in her marriage nor did He prevent her from making a bad decision or spending time in a king's harem. During her walk, a loving God said "no" to some things. Yet, she chose to trust Him rather than submit to fear. And God rewarded her faith with an outpouring of His blessing in other ways.

Likewise, God may not choose to rescue you from poor decisions made by you or someone close to you or those circumstances of life beyond your control that bring you pain. But in any and all situations, you can count on these truths…

#1. God loves me
#2. God knows what is going on in my life
#3. God can do something about it
#4. I can trust His goodness in whatever He chooses to do

That is your walk from fear to faith.

JOURNAL YOUR FAITH STORY

Consider poor decisions made by you or someone close to you that have brought fear into your life. How did you respond? What have you learned that could help you respond with even more faith in God in your future?

FAITH IN ACTION

"PRESS ON BEYOND ANY WEAKNESS"

Recommended: Listen to the podcast "Sarah-Press on Beyond Your Weaknesses." Use the section below as a listener guide.

What happens when something goes wrong in your life? You know, not the way you planned or imagined. Do you feel dazed, embarrassed, or angry?

You may look at your life and only see weaknesses. You feel helpless as a victim of circumstances. You dwell on your mistakes. You focus on your inadequacies, not being enough of...whatever. And sadly, other people like to point out all those weaknesses in your life, too, making you feel even worse about them.

God calls us to live by faith. Faith involves trust in a God who loves us, who cares, who can guide us, but who has not promised to remove all the obstacles in our paths. And He knows about our weaknesses.

Jesus is able to empathize with our weaknesses because He knows what we are going through. So we can go to Him with confidence and get help in our time of need (Hebrews 4:15-16). Paul wrote that the Spirit of God helps us in our weakness in accordance with God's will for our lives (Romans 8:26-27).

Our God has bigger purposes for our weaknesses than what we can see or know each step of the way. He knows what causes us fear. It does not matter if our fear is driven by circumstances we cannot fix, stems from making mistakes, or is caused by feelings of inadequacy. Our God is bigger than our weaknesses. He asks us to trust Him and His purpose when we don't understand.

God is bigger than your circumstances

> Circumstances = those conditions affecting our lives that are beyond our control or ability to "fix."

Think of Sarah's circumstances. Her barrenness was out of her control. She did not do anything wrong. And in her specific case, God had a bigger plan for her that depended on the right timing, which she knew nothing about. Sarah endured long periods of drought, which brought on the famine, which caused Abraham to go to Egypt to find grazing land for his herds, where she ended up in Pharaoh's harem. That famine was not her fault. She did not do anything wrong. Yet, she suffered.

You may be facing your own version of desperate circumstances—health problems, lack of income, bad relationships, or something someone else has caused. Having to face those circumstances leaves you with choices. You can become whiny and bitter. Or you can depend upon God to get you through them. It is even likely that you will learn to see and appreciate God's gifts to you in a greater way. God is bigger than your circumstances. If He was not bigger than your circumstances, He would not be God.

God is bigger than your mistakes

Mistakes = 1) Willfully going against clear Biblical guidance about what is right and wrong. 2) Attempting to "fix a problem," without clear Biblical guidance. When it does not turn out as expected, we can regret that decision as a "mistake."

Sarah made one gigantic mistake in her life that is recorded for everyone to know and point fingers at her. She took something acceptable from her culture and tried to use it to obtain the promise of God. That mistake had huge, painful consequences. But God's purpose was not thwarted because of her mistake. She experienced God's graciousness to her and gave birth to Isaac. I bet everyone within earshot of Sarah for the rest of her life heard this marvelous story of God's faithfulness to her.

But what about those things not clearly defined as right and wrong in the Bible—where you live, where you work, or where to invest money? God has given us a mind to use for making decisions in those areas of life. So we should pray, ask for guidance from the Holy Spirit, get advice from other believers, check to see if it is legal, then make the decision and act on it.

Living by faith includes the whole process of trusting God while making a decision and trusting God with the results of it. It is all about faith—not about being perfect. God is bigger than your mistakes. If He was not bigger than your mistakes, He would not be God.

God is bigger than your inadequacies

> Inadequate = failing to reach an expected or required standard,
> to be insufficient and lacking

Some of us wallow in our inadequacies. God knows all about those things in which we feel insufficient and lacking. Sometimes, He leaves us to ourselves so we will recognize how insufficient we are without Him. Then, we will desire Him more. Have you noticed this in your life?

Sarah was inadequate in her barrenness. And I think she had lost hope. Have you ever lost hope? The angel of the Lord appeared and personally gave her the good news she would soon be a mother. Sarah laughed, was confronted by the angel, became afraid and lied about her laughter. But God did not zap her. Instead, He rejuvenated her body and filled it with the long-promised son.

Thankfully, God has compassion on our inadequacies. What do you feel is inadequate in your life? I am not talking about material things right now, but where do you feel you lack as a person? Your character, your abilities. God is bigger than your inadequacies. If He was not bigger than your inadequacies, He would not be God.

The apostle Paul knew he had dragged Christians to prison to be beaten and killed. But he also knew God was bigger than his past, so he wrote in Philippians these words,

> *But one thing I do: Forgetting what is behind and straining*
> *toward what is ahead, I press on... (Philippians 3:13-14)*

Press on beyond any weakness

So instead of responding to desperate circumstances with hysteria, or replaying mistakes over and over in your mind, or wallowing in your inadequacies, **what are you going to do today to move forward?** Beyond circumstances you are in. Beyond mistakes you have made. Beyond any feelings of inadequacy that you have.

How will you trust God now to show you how to press on toward a new future? And as you press on, you can count on these 4 truths that are not nullified by your weaknesses.

#1. God loves me
#2. God knows what is going on in my life

#3. God can do something about it

#4. I can trust His goodness in whatever He chooses to do

We have a big God. He can take whatever is looking ugly in our lives and make it something praiseworthy. Maybe all that you have been through in life—desperate circumstances, blaring mistakes, and obvious inadequacies—have led to this moment when God has brought you to hear this message and trust in Him. God is bigger than your weaknesses. He could be showing you that today.

REFLECT

Reread Philippians 3:12-14. Take just one of the questions below and apply what you just read to it. How will you press on, trusting in God?

1) Have you faced desperate **circumstances**, maybe because of health problems, consequences of someone else's sin, or relationships that have failed?

2) Do you live in fear of making **mistakes** or of others making mistakes that affect you? Have you made a big mistake with unwelcome consequences?

3) What do you feel is **inadequate** in your life? Not just material things, but where do you feel you lack as a person?

What are you going to do today to trust God and press on beyond that weakness?

Pray about your fears and decisions you are making to trust God in them. Thank God for His grace toward you and His love for you.

3 God Is Stronger than Your Enemies

BY FAITH...JOCHEBED & MIRIAM

By faith Moses' parents hid him for three months after he was born, because they saw he was no ordinary child, and they were not afraid of the king's edict. HEBREWS 11:23

I brought you up out of Egypt and redeemed you from the land of slavery. I sent Moses to lead you, also Aaron and Miriam. MICAH 6:4

> Pray: Lord Jesus, please teach me through this lesson.

A little bit of history

The descendants of Sarah and Abraham became the Israelites (also called Hebrews) who settled in Egypt for 430 years. At first, their presence was welcome because the "vice president" of the country was their relative Joseph. But after Joseph died, Pharaohs ruled who did not know Joseph. Fearing the Hebrews' might, Egypt sought to cripple the growing nation, but those efforts were in vain. God was with His people, and He was preparing to bring Israel out of the land.

Conservative scholars date "the Exodus," a landmark in Israel's history, at 1446 B.C. Moses was born 80 years earlier, just after a decree to throw newborn Hebrew boys into the Nile. But he escaped death when he was adopted by Pharaoh's daughter. By age 40, Moses began to defend the Hebrews. Pharaoh tried to kill him, but Moses escaped to Midian. Forty years later, the Lord appeared to Moses in a burning bush, sending Moses back to Egypt to confront the current Pharaoh.

Through Moses, God showed Pharaoh who was the true God and brought Egypt to her knees. The Israelites marched forth a free people, living proof of God's gracious salvation. At Mount Sinai, God molded His people into a nation—Israel. The Mosaic Covenant contained laws that governed every part of Israel's society: civil, religious, and moral. Though some people rebelled against God, He faithfully preserved a new generation of His people through the wilderness. Moses' mother Jochebed and sister Miriam were influential women during this time.

Miriam's childhood and her mentors

Read Numbers 26:59.

Who were the members of Miriam's family?

Read Exodus 1:15-22.

Over several generations, God used brave women to thwart evil plans to eliminate His people.

Who were the women in this chapter exhibiting courage, and what did they do (verses 15-19)?

What did God do for them (verses 20-21)?

These women who had courage were "mentors" for Jochebed and her daughter Miriam.

Read Exodus 2:1-10.

What do you learn about Miriam's mom, Jochebed?

What choices did Miriam's parents (Jochebed and Amram) make because of their faith?

How did God reward that faith (verses 9 and 10)?

Miriam is the sister mentioned in this passage (7-12 years of age). As a young girl, what fearful situations did Miriam face?

How did she respond to them?

Read Hebrews 11:23-28.

What influence did the few years spent with his family have on Moses?

Miriam had the same home and parents as Moses. Moses, Aaron, and Miriam came from a home where parents were walking by faith in their God. This influence helped their children learn to courageously trust God and not give way to fear.

Consider the kind of home in which you grew up. How has this affected your ability to courageously trust God and not give way to fear?

Here was a mother who faced a very real danger (mine is imagined), and yet she trusted God. Her faith was put into action. When we take what we learn in the Word and then turn it into faith-in-action, fear loses its grip on our hearts and we are not only able to live in victory and experience God's abounding peace, but we become a living example to our children. (Shirley Ann Vels, "Under an English Sky" blog, July 30, 2013)

Miriam - 80 years later

Miriam is now in her upper mid-life, ~87-92 years old! According to Jewish tradition, Miriam's husband was Hur, an honorable man who joined Aaron to hold up Moses' arms during a major battle in Exodus 17 and was appointed as a magistrate while Moses was on the mountain (Exodus 24:14).

Read Micah 6:4.

What does God say about Miriam's role for Israel?

After the Israelites left Egypt, they traveled east for several days. While camped by the Red Sea, they began to panic when they saw Pharaoh's army coming after them. But God's faithfulness would shine in what He did for them next.

Read Exodus 14:10-31.

Along with the rest of Israel, what did Miriam experience that showed God's faithfulness?

Read Exodus 15:18-21.

Moses led the people in a praise song (Exodus 15:1-18). What did Miriam do as a leader (verses 20-21)?

Miriam acted as a leader of the women in praising God, fulfilling His purpose for her (Micah 6:4).

What is Miriam called in Exodus 15:20?

Miriam was a female prophet—one to whom and through whom God speaks, revealing Himself and His will especially in the absence of the written word of God. God used a number of women to speak forth His Word at critical times in history—for example, Deborah (Judges 4-5) and Huldah (2 Kings 22).

Prophesying also could involve an enthusiastic praising of God inspired by the Holy Spirit. Such praise involved singing, dancing, and playing musical instruments as here in Exodus 15. This song is the first recorded song in the Bible—a song of redemption. Such celebration was common after victory in battle.

About 2 years later

Read Numbers 12:1-15.

What complaint did Miriam and Aaron have regarding Moses (verse 2)?

How did the Lord respond to their behavior (verses 4-10)?

What is implied by the Lord's punishment of Miriam only?

How did the two brothers respond to their sister's discipline (verses 11-13)?

What was God's answer (verse 14)?

According to Deuteronomy 25:9, spitting in someone's face expressed contempt. The Lord expressed His contempt for Miriam's disrespect by the skin affliction, causing her to live outside the community until healed (Numbers 5:1-4). Miriam bucked her authority, claiming equal prominence with Moses. God disciplined her through banishment, opposite of what she really wanted!

Knowing women, what was likely the effect of Miriam's banishment from the camp for 7 days on her?

Sometimes Miriam was a good example. Sometimes she was a bad example. Just like we are, she was not perfect every day. Yet, she had been given a sphere of influence by God. She lived through 38 years of wandering and died at ~130 years old (Numbers 20:1) in their 40th year out of Egypt.

Read Hebrews 13:17.

What should be our attitude towards authority that represents God?

Though all of us are not leaders, all of us are under some kind of authority in the Church. Fear of losing our status or influence can lead us to be disrespectful to those in spiritual authority over us. If you are jealous, resentful, or disapproving of someone in leadership over you, consider whether you try to undermine their leadership by gossip or slander. Ask Jesus to help you stop that today.

THE WALK FROM FEAR TO FAITH

Consider the situations that could have terrified Jochebed. How did she respond to God by faith?

What situations could have terrified Miriam? How did she respond to God by faith?

God loved Miriam's family. He knew what was going on in their lives. He was able to do something about it. But God did not give Jochebed her son back permanently to raise nor did He prevent them from having to go through the agony of hiding baby Moses. Miriam was given great responsibility and privilege, yet she also had to live with the public consequences of her sin. During her walk, a loving God said "no" to some things. Yet, Miriam and her family chose to trust Him rather than submit to fear. And God rewarded their faith with an outpouring of His blessing in other ways.

Likewise, God may not choose to rescue you from your "Egypt." But in any and all situations, you can count on these truths...

#1. God loves me
#2. God knows what is going on in my life
#3. God can do something about it
#4. I can trust His goodness in whatever He chooses to do

That is your walk from fear to faith.

Journal Your Faith Story

Miriam testified about God's faithfulness through her use of poetry, song, and dance. Since the day of Pentecost, the Holy Spirit living in believers continues to inspire and gift believers to compose songs, poems, prayers, and testimonies that glorify God. Praise helps us to overcome fear.

> *Maybe you have written a song, a poem, created a work of art, or simply sung praise songs to God. Share about a time when you broke out into spontaneous praise to God in one of these ways or another way.*

FAITH IN ACTION

"APPLY FAITH TO FEAR"

Recommended: *Listen to the podcast "Miriam-How to Apply Faith to Any Fear." Use the section below as a listener guide.*

Miriam experienced that amazing exit from Egypt along with more than 2 million others. When the people were terrified, the Lord fought for them. They needed only to stop being terrified and trust Him. Through Moses' instructions, the trembling people were able to apply faith to their fear. They confronted it and turned it over to God. Their faithful God took over, proving that He was stronger than their enemies.

Here is a biblical tool that you can use to apply faith to any fear.

STEP 1. **Confront** *it. What fears do you have right now?*

List the things that make you afraid. The real fears and the imaginary ones. Which ones are the most likely to tempt you to panic or to be terrified? Focus on those.

STEP 2. **Ask** *about each one: What is my worst-case scenario?*

Start with one fear and ask, "What is the worst that could happen?" Think realistically not hypothetically.

STEP 3. **Consider**: *If the worst I can imagine happens, could I handle it through the presence and power of Jesus Christ?*

As a Christian, you have the power of the One who created the Universe living inside of you. Ask yourself, "Can He help me get through anything?" The answer is a resounding, "YES!" *Hebrews 4:15-16; Ephesians 3:20; Romans 8:26*

STEP 4. **Remember** *the four truths essential to faith:*

#1. God loves me. *John 16:27; Romans 5:5, Ephesians 5:1*
#2. God knows what is going on in my life. *Matthew 6:31-32; Psalm 139:1-10*
#3. God can do something about it. *Genesis 18:14; Luke 1:37; Mark 10:27*
#4. I can trust His goodness in whatever He chooses to do. *Psalm 119:68; Proverbs 3:5*

STEP 5. **Pray**: *Prayer is simply talking to God about anything and everything.*

- Thank the Lord for His presence and His goodness and anything else that comes to mind. *1 Thessalonians 5:18*

- Ask Him for the courage and peace to ride out the storm. Where the Bible is clear, you can claim God's promises by faith—such as the promise of peace. *John 14:27; 16:33*

- Anytime, you can ask for deliverance and protection—but you cannot hold God to promises He has not made. He has not promised immunity from natural calamities, from illness, or from troubles.

STEP 6. **Live life** *securely in Him: What actions can you take?*

- Take common sense precautions. Be wise in the world. *Nehemiah 4:9*

- Trust God to show you what to do and give you strength when you are weak.

You can find a copy of this tool at the end of this study guide. Snap a picture to keep it on your phone, or cut it out and keep in your Bible so you can apply faith to any fear.

REFLECT

Work through these steps to apply faith to one of your most pressing fears.

Pray about your fears and decisions you are making to trust God in them. Thank God for His grace toward you and His love for you.

God Is Good in the Waiting

BY FAITH ... RAHAB

By faith the prostitute Rahab, because she welcomed the spies, was not killed with those who were disobedient. HEBREWS 11:31

> Pray: Lord Jesus, please teach me through this lesson.

A little bit of history

After 40 years of struggle, Israel stood poised to cross the Jordan River and enter the Promised Land around 1400 BC. But she would enter without Moses for he was dead. This beautiful new land was dangerous. Numerous city-states dotted the landscape—each a walled fortress with a battle-tested army. Conquest would be difficult and time-consuming.

But a faithful God equipped a new leader named Joshua who had been trained under Moses' leadership for many years for this job. Joshua knew that the 2 million Israelites plus their flocks and herds needed to cross a flooded river to begin their conquest of the land. So he sent 2 spies to secretly scout the area of Jericho, the strategic point to reach the three passes through the wilderness to the rest of Canaan. God miraculously provided dry ground for the Israelites to cross the Jordan River. A few miles away was Jericho, a walled city covering 9½ acres. One trip around the city could have taken less than an hour.

Read Deuteronomy 4:32-35.

Why were the Israelites shown so many miraculous things (verse 35)?

Read Deuteronomy 2:24-25.

How would God use fear to His advantage?

Getting to know Rahab

Read Joshua 2:1-11.

What did Rahab and the people of Jericho know about Israel and her history (verses 9-10)?

As a result, what was the state of morale in Jericho (verse 11)?

The state of morale in Jericho was going according to God's plan (Deuteronomy 2:25). Their hearts "melted in fear." Isn't that a vivid word picture? Have you ever melted in fear?

According to archeological excavations, the citizens of Jericho were well prepared for a siege. A spring provided water inside the city walls, and the harvest had just been gathered providing an abundant supply of food (Joshua 3:15). So the inhabitants of Jericho could have held out for perhaps several years. Large jars full of grain found in the remains of houses show that the siege was short since the people had consumed very little of the grain. This is verification of the Bible's accuracy regarding history.

In verses 1-11, what do you learn about Rahab as a woman?

Here is a woman who is a business woman, gutsy, quick-thinking, shows kindness, is proactive for herself and her family, and is resourceful. You probably know some women like that, although maybe not in her line of business (prostitute). ☺

What conclusion did Rahab make about the God of Israel (verse 11)?

Could anyone else in Jericho have come to the same conclusion?

The conclusion that Rahab made about the God of Israel was exactly what God wanted all of them to know (Deuteronomy 4:35). Everyone heard the same news. While most stayed in their fear, Rahab responded with faith to the revelation given. Rahab was given an opportunity to make a conscious choice for God based upon the few facts she knew about Him, and she responded with FAITH. Faith resulted in action.

What actions did she take to protect the spies (verses 4-7)?

Read Joshua 2:12-21.

What did Rahab ask of the spies (verses 12-13)?

The spies made a covenant with Rahab. What part of the oath was Rahab's responsibility (verses 17-20)?

What part of the oath was the responsibility of the spies?

How did she help the spies escape (verses 15-16)?

Rahab transferred her allegiance to God and Israel. She asked for kindness while also showing kindness as she first protected the spies and then assisted in their escape. Rahab agreed to the terms of the covenant. She likely tied that scarlet cord in the window right away then moved her family to her house within 3 days. She risked being found out by the king and punished, facing ridicule from her family, perhaps being called a traitor, and worst of all being forgotten by the spies when Israel attacked. That would have been devastating to her!

The spies returned to camp. God parted the Jordan River for the people to cross. The men who had been born in the wilderness were circumcised. The Passover was celebrated. And the people ate produce from the land. The manna stopped the next day.

Read Joshua 6:1-25.

What was God's plan for defeating Jericho (verses 2-5)?

How did Joshua and the people respond (verses 6-15)?

Rahab had to wait those seven days also. Based on her responsibility in the oath, who else was waiting with her?

***What might have been Rahab's emotions during this time
of waiting?***

Having all those family members waiting with her (mother, father
and brothers with their families) meant that she was feeding them
and keeping them focused on possible rescue rather than
destruction. Can you imagine how hard that might have been!

Did you consider she might have worried that the red cord would
not be seen? Maybe she worried that she would be forgotten. Do
you worry that God may have forgotten you? I think she might have
had some impatience, too. When would the attack take place? Is
today the day? She was not privy to God's plan. Do you ever get
impatient for God to work? I sure do. She was definitely not in
control of anything except keeping her family with her.

Someone once said, "Responsibility is my response to His (God's)
ability." Rahab responded to God's ability. She made sure that
scarlet cord was hanging in plain sight so she could be found.

***Joshua's name means "salvation." How was God faithful
to Rahab through Joshua so that she and her family were
saved (verses 17, 22-25)?***

Archaeologists have found that surrounding Jericho was a great earthen
embankment with a stone retaining wall at its base 12–15 feet high.
Above that stood a mud brick wall 6 feet thick, 20 feet high. At the crest
of the embankment was a similar 20-foot high mud brick wall reaching
to 46 feet above the ground level below. There were houses built against
the wall as in Joshua 2:15. Evidence reveals that the mud brick city wall
collapsed at the time the city met its end **except for a short stretch of
the north city wall that did not fall as everywhere else.** Could this
have been Rahab's part of the wall? Excavations showed that the bricks
from the collapsed walls formed a ramp against the retaining wall so that
the Israelites could climb up over the top as is described in Joshua 6:20.
The city was thoroughly burned.

Read Matthew 1:5.

What information is given about Rahab?

Read Hebrews 11:30, 31.

What information is given about Rahab?

In Hebrews 11:31, the word "disobedient" is used to describe the rest of the people of Jericho. The original Greek word means, "to refuse to be persuaded." God had given all the people ample opportunity to be persuaded, but they refused. Do you know someone like that?

Read James 2:25.

Why was Rahab considered righteous to the Jews?

God's grace to Rahab forgave her past and gave her a new future. She was given a place among the Israelites as a recognizable person because she acted on faith instead of melting into fear. She married an Israelite man and produced a son who was King David's great grandfather, placing Rahab in the lineage of our Lord Jesus.

For centuries, Christians have tried to soften Rahab's reputation by arguing that she was only an innkeeper, but the New Testament references to her indicate that she was an immoral woman. The Greek word used to describe Rahab is "porne" the word from which we get "pornography." "Porne" is only used for immorality. This in no way mars the righteousness of God who used such a person in the fulfillment of His purposes. Instead this incident serves to bring His mercy and grace into bold relief. (Adapted from *The Bible Knowledge Commentary, Old Testament,* page 330)

You may feel that some sins in your past or present are so terrible that they cannot be forgiven or that you are unworthy to serve God.

What have you learned from Rahab's story reminding you that God can forgive your past and give you a new future?

THE WALK FROM FEAR TO FAITH

List the opportunities for fear in Rahab's life.

How did she demonstrate faith at those times?

God loved Rahab. He knew what was going on in her life. He was able to do something about it. But God did not keep Rahab from losing the security of her home nor did He prevent her from having to go through the agony of watching the Israelites march around the city for 7 days. Remember, she did not know that plan. When she stepped out in faith, He met her there. She trusted Him to rescue her, and He did. God judged her by her heart not by her lifestyle. He not only saved her life, but He forgave her past and gave her a new future. She chose to trust Him rather than melt in fear.

Likewise, God forgives your past and gives you a new future. And in any and all situations, you can count on these truths...

#1. God loves me
#2. God knows what is going on in my life
#3. God can do something about it
#4. I can trust His goodness in whatever He chooses to do

That is your walk from fear to faith.

Journal Your Faith Story

We will probably never be faced with the dramatic circumstances of Rahab, but we do have our own distressing situations in life. Rahab had to wait patiently for God to act. Remember that she did not know the "marching" orders. We also must wait for God to answer our petitions. And these times of waiting strengthen our relationship with Him as we learn to rely on His timing and trust in His goodness. Read the words to the song below.

> You are in the waiting in that moment of my life, when my faith and hope collide. My heart's anticipating just how and when You'll move. Oh, that is when You prove You are in the waiting too (Shannon Wexelberg, "In the Waiting")

Is waiting a problem for you? Have you become discouraged (or been discouraged in the past) from having to wait? Look back on that time and consider ways you can recognize that God was in the waiting, too.

FAITH IN ACTION

"TRUST GOD'S GOODNESS"

Recommended: *Listen to the podcast "Rahab-God Is Good All the Time." Use the section below as a listener guide.*

By faith, Rahab made a conscious choice to wait and depend on her new God to rescue her. Most of us don't like to wait for God to work. And we say to each other, "God is good all the time," but do we really believe that when we have to wait?

KEY TRUTH: God is good all the time

You are good, and what you do is good; (Psalm 119:68)

The Bible reveals that everything about God is good—He is good in Himself, and what He does is good. That means God allows nothing to happen to His children that is not for their good. God is good all the time, and He is at work in our lives for good.

God's goodness has three aspects that apply to times of fear and pain: 1) He is good even in the tough times; 2) He is good in different ways to each of us, and 3) He is good in what He allows or does not allow in our lives.

1) God is good even in the tough times

God teaches His children through tough things He allows in our lives that help us grow up and build bones and teeth in our faith. They help us learn to trust God and give up trying to do things our own way—which may not be the best way—and start doing things God's way—which is always the best way. ANYTHING that draws us closer to God and makes us depend upon Him is good for us.

2) God is good in different ways to each of us

God's goodness looks different in each person's life. In the book of Ruth, Naomi and her family were starving so they moved away from Israel to the neighboring country Moab to get bread. There they met Ruth who did not need bread. She needed God. Naomi shared God with Ruth. Different needs were met by God's goodness.

3) *God is good in what He allows or does not allow into our lives*

Not everyone gets cancer, has a serious injury or chronic illness, endures long-term unemployment, loses a child, or experiences the desertion of a spouse. We don't even know all the dangers God is protecting us from daily! We should consider the bad things that He does not allow into our lives and thank Him all the time for doing that.

Trust His Choosing and Depend on Him

Do you believe that God has the right to choose what He brings into your life? It is **your choice** to TRUST **His choice** of how to be good to you. Anything that makes us depend on Him is good for us.

We cannot move from fear to faith on our own. We must depend on God's Spirit-power in us.

- Fear says, "I can't." Faith says, "God can through me."
- Fear says, "I won't." Faith says, "God will in me."
- Fear says, "I don't." Faith says, "God does for me."

Say about anything, "Lord Jesus, I cannot do this on my own. But you can do this in and through me. I will trust you." And it is okay to be a little scared because you will rely upon Him more.

Even while you are waiting for God to answer a desperate prayer, count on the fact that God is good all the time. Embrace these 4 truths to sustain you in the waiting as you walk from fear to faith.

#1 God loves me.
#2 God knows what is going on in my life.
#3 God can do something about it.
#4 I can **trust His goodness** in whatever He chooses to do!

REFLECT

Consider painful circumstances that have driven you to rely upon God. What did you learn about His goodness through that experience?

Pray about your fears and decisions you are making to trust God in them. Thank God for His grace toward you and His love for you.

5 God's Riches Meet Your Needs

Fear to FAITH

BY FAITH...TWO SINGLE MOMS

So do not worry, saying, "What shall we eat?" or "What shall we drink?" or "What shall we wear?" For the pagans run after all these things, and your heavenly Father knows that you need them. But seek first his kingdom and his righteousness, and all these things will be given to you as well. Therefore, do not worry about tomorrow, for tomorrow will worry about itself. Each day has enough trouble of its own. MATTHEW 6:31-34

> Pray: Lord Jesus, please teach me through this lesson.

A little bit of history

David reigned on Israel's throne for 40 years. His son Solomon became famous for his God-given wisdom, strengthened Israel's defenses, conducted trade throughout the known world, and engaged in numerous building operations including a magnificent temple for God. But his foreign wives turned his heart away from God, so God judged this sin by dividing the Kingdom after his death. Solomon's son Rehoboam reigned over Judah—the southern kingdom (2 tribes—Judah and Benjamin). Jeroboam (a general) was made king over Israel—the northern kingdom (the other 10 tribes). But Jeroboam rebelled against God and established a substitute religious system that turned the people away from their God. Sin always brings judgment. In 722 BC, God allowed the Assyrians to destroy Samaria, Israel's capital, bringing the Northern Kingdom to an end.

During this tumultuous time, God called men and women to become His *prophet*—to receive messages directly from God and proclaim them to both kings and ordinary people. Unlike the priest or the king, the prophet did not inherit his office. He received his calling directly from God. Some, like Elijah, were called into a lifetime of service to God, while others performed one simple, yet important, job.

About 150 years before the end of the Northern Kingdom, two single moms lived who were struggling just to survive. Things looked hopeless.

Recall a time in your life when God creatively provided for you as things looked hopeless. What was it like?

GETTING TO KNOW THE WIDOW OF ZAREPHATH

The town of Zarephath was located between Tyre and Sidon in modern Lebanon. Being Gentile territory, the people worshiped the idol Baal. Elijah was sent to Zarephath to a widow whom God had already chosen to receive His help although she was not Jewish. God's grace and mercy is always available to individuals. Let us call this widow 'Zee.'

Read 1 Kings 17:1-16.

What was 'Zee's' crisis situation, and how was she planning to deal with it (verses 10-12)?

What might have been her emotions at this time?

What did Elijah ask of 'Zee' (verse 13)?

What did God promise to do for her (verse 14)?

How did 'Zee' respond (first part of 15)?

How was God faithful to His promise (verses 15-16)?

Only a true God can provide flour and oil in a drought! Elijah stayed with the widow and her son, eating flour and oil cakes twice a day for almost 3 years! How long could you stay grateful while eating the same meal twice a day for 3 years?!

Read 1 Kings 17:17-24.

What was 'Zee's' crisis now (verse 17)?

How did she respond to the crisis (verse 18)?

'Zee's' response is a common reaction among people who do not know God's ways when personal tragedy hits their lives. It is the pagan view of life: "When things go well, the gods are pleased with me. When things go wrong, the gods are angry with me." But Jesus said in Matthew 5:45 that God sends sunshine and rain on both the righteous and the unrighteous equally. For 'Zee,' it was God's opportunity to take her another step along her faith walk, making it personal. Elijah took the boy to his upstairs room and pleaded with God to restore his life.

What did God do (verse 22)?

How did 'Zee's' faith grow as a result of God's faithfulness to her (verse 24)?

The living God showed His goodness to her through Elijah's presence, daily food supply, and restoration of her son. 'Zee' responded with personal faith in Him.

GETTING TO KNOW THE PROPHET'S WIDOW

Elijah served as God's prophet in Israel for many years. He mentored a local farmer named Elisha to help him and to continue the ministry after Elijah was taken to heaven (2 Kings 2). Three characteristics distinguished God's true prophet: 1) he was loyal to God alone, 2) his predictions came true, and 3) his message agreed with previous revelations. Performing miracles was not the primary test because false prophets could do that through Satan's power (Deuteronomy 13:1-2).

Read 2 Kings 4:1-7.

Let us call this widow 'PW.' 'PW's' husband was a member of a school of prophets similar to Bible schools. One community of prophets was located at Bethel, just north of Jerusalem. The Mosaic Law provided for paying off debts by working but with limitations (Leviticus 25:39-41). God gave instructions to His people to continually care for the needy, especially widows and orphans (Deuteronomy 24:19-22). By the time these two women lived, widows and orphans were not only neglected and ignored, they were also oppressed and cheated. But our faithful God "defends the cause of the fatherless and the widow (Deuteronomy 10:18)."

What was 'PW's' crisis situation, and how did she deal with it (verse 1)?

What did Elisha as God's representative ask her (verse 2)?

Then, what did he direct 'PW' to do (verses 3-4)?

How did 'PW' and her boys respond (verses 5-6)?

How did God provide for this family's current and future needs (verse 7)?

Olive oil was expensive and time-consuming to make. It was used for cooking, lighting lamps, dressing wounds, and as a deodorant when water was not available for bathing. The wealthy used it for a skin softener. It was also used for anointing kings and the dead for burial as well as for ritual offerings. The widow had a valuable commodity that she likely sold back to her neighbors.

Elisha told 'PW' to ask her neighbors for jars (verse 3). What could have been the benefits of doing this?

How could this incident have impacted her sons?

Consider the kind of help 'PW' had sought from God and what she received. How did God defend her cause?

We often overlook what God has already provided for us and concentrate instead on what we don't have. In this lesson, God used what both 'Zee' and 'PW' already had as a resource to multiply on their behalf. If you have someone in your sphere of influence who is a widow, single mom, or otherwise needy, be her advocate and help her to look at her resources. Then, join her in asking God to multiply what she already has to meet her needs. This would include yourself as well.

THE WALK FROM FEAR TO FAITH

Consider the fearful situations that 'Zee' faced. How did she respond to God with faith?

Consider the fearful situations that 'PW' faced. How did she respond to God with faith?

God loved the two single moms and their children. He knew what was going on in their lives. He was able to do something about it. But God did not restore their husbands back to these women nor did He prevent them from going through the agony of watching food supplies dwindle or facing threats from a creditor. His provision was not luxurious foods or easy money. During their walk, a loving God said no to some things. Yet, they chose to trust Him rather than submit to fear. And God rewarded their faith with an outpouring of His blessing. Likewise, God may not choose to remove the threats from your life. But in any and all situations, you can count on these truths...

#1. God loves me
#2. God knows what is going on in my life
#3. God can do something about it
#4. I can trust His goodness in whatever He chooses to do

That is your walk from fear to faith.

Journal Your Faith Walk

Reflect on the words of the song below. Search on YouTube to listen to it.

Had a lot of dreams that never came true. Things I could have done, but never got the chance to do. When I couldn't see the path of the storm your wisdom wouldn't let me go that way. And it broke my heart, but now my heart can say,

Thank you for the times you said, No. Thank you for the doors that you closed. All the ways you never let me go and the things you never gave me. So many times I did not understand and wouldn't let you take my hand. But now I want to fall at Your feet and thank you for the things you never gave me. (David Meece, "Things You Never Gave Me")

How grateful are you for the times when God says, "No?" Consider an experience where God did not respond as you hoped He would. How did you react? What was the ultimate outcome? What did you learn about God?

"RECOGNIZE GOD'S PROVISION"

Recommended: *Listen to the podcast "Two Widows-Recognize God's Provision." Use the section below as a listener guide.*

Jesus said to His followers, "Don't let your needs dominate your thoughts." Your heavenly Father knows your needs. Give yourself to the Lord first. **Think differently about God's provision for you**. God has 4 lessons for us to learn regarding His provision to us.

Lesson #1: God's provision is His to give and take away. Regard it humbly.

• *Everything we have comes from God.*

There is not anything we have that we did not receive from God—birthplace, height, attractiveness, intelligence, natural talents (1 Corinthians 4:7). Yet we live as though we had something to do with those things.

• *What we have is not a measure of our goodness or our faith.*

How God chooses to provide for you or for me at any time in our lives is His sovereign choice. When God removes our comforts and strips away our support, we actually begin to depend on Him as God Almighty—as an **essential to our lives**, not just an appendage. Do not let anyone deceive you by equating prosperity with your measure of faith.

• *God determines our provision—the how, when, and why*

Most of the time, God's provision is going to come through people, not miraculously appear from the sky. People design products and services to sell. They take the risk to start businesses and hire workers, including you. People buy farmers' crops. And people provide meals for someone in a time of need. We must learn to trust whatever manner He chooses.

• *Our provision belongs to God. Hold onto it loosely.*

Just before Elijah went to live with 'Zee,' God placed him beside a stream for 6 months. Birds brought him food twice a day (1 Kings 17:1-6). But it is during a drought, so he watches the stream gradually dry up!

The God who gave the water has chosen to take the water. It is His sovereign right! He gives the child; He can take it away. He gives the business; He can take it away. He gives the house; He can take it away. (Chuck Swindoll, sermon series on Elijah)

Lesson #2: God's provision is always enough. Receive it gratefully.

• *The sufficiency of God's enough*

After 40 years of life in the desert, eating just morning manna and evening quail, without house, farm, new shoes, or clothes, Moses tells the people of Israel they "lacked nothing" (Deuteronomy 2:7). Later, he tells them that in their new land with abundant water and bountiful food they "will lack nothing" (Deuteronomy 8:7-9). When you have the Lord's provision (whatever it is), you lack nothing that you need at this time in your life. It is what you HAVE that counts, not what you do not have.

• *The creativity of God's enough*

When you receive God's provision, you learn that He is trustworthy, creative, and personal. For 'Zee,' she had endless pancakes but only enough for today with a promise for tomorrow. She had to trust that flour bucket to be refilled for the next day's meals. She lacked nothing. For 'PW,' she had a bottomless pot of oil, enough for today and to plan for her future. She lacked nothing. God does not do the same thing for everyone. Your hope is to be in your God, not in prosperity—current or future.

Lesson #3: God's provision is meant to be shared. Give it generously.

• *Compassion is doing, not feeling*

Compassion is doing something to ease someone's pain, whether it is for this week or more. It is proactive. God's plan for the needy was that perfectly good food was **purposely** left in the fields for the poor to have.

• *Compassion requires trusting God, not having plenty*

A fine line exists between good stewardship of the provisions given today and not trusting God enough to be able to share it. It is what you do with what you have. God gave us a wonderful example to follow in the Macedonian Christians.

Out of the most severe trial, their overflowing joy and their extreme poverty welled up in rich generosity... they gave themselves first to the Lord and then to us in keeping with God's will. (2 Corinthians 8:2, 7)

• *Compassion shares God's riches flowing through us*

God's grace can make a dynamic difference in the mindset of His people when it comes to provision. How you respond as the receiver or the giver should be **different** than what the world does. God's riches to us are supplied through us to meet another's needs (2 Corinthians 8:13-14).

• *Compassion is personal*

Have you experienced the joy of deliberately and delightfully meeting the specific needs of a person with a name and a face you know? Compassion is personal.

Lesson #4: God's provision brings Him glory. Praise Him openly.

Acknowledge that what we have, whether much or little, all comes from God. Ask God to give you frequent opportunity to tell your story. That gives Him glory. Recognize God's provision to you is being supplied to you for His purposes. Whenever there does not seem to be enough, remember these four truths to stand strong in the tough times:

#1. God loves me
#2. God knows what is going on in my life
#3. God can do something about it
#4. I can trust His goodness in whatever He chooses to do

REFLECT

What did you learn from this faith-in-action that helps you walk from fear to faith regarding God's provision for you?

Pray about your fears and decisions you are making to trust God in them. Thank God for His grace toward you and His love for you.

Trusting God? Tell It!

By Faith...The Shunammite Woman

The king was talking to Gehazi, the servant of the man of God, and had said, "Tell me about all the great things Elisha has done." Just as Gehazi was telling the king how Elisha had restored the dead to life, the woman whose son Elisha had brought back to life came to appeal to the king for her house and land. Gehazi said, "This is the woman, my lord the king, and this is her son whom Elisha restored to life." The king asked the woman about it, and she told him. Then he assigned an official to her case and said to him, "Give back everything that belonged to her, including all the income from her land from the day she left the country until now." 2 Kings 8:4-6a

> Pray: Lord Jesus, please teach me through this lesson.

A little bit of history

God's concern for women and their special needs is clearly seen in the Bible. Whereas women were regarded as inferior to men in most ancient Near Eastern societies, God demonstrated His compassion for them in dynamic, recognizable ways. Times were hard, though. Famines were common. The kings were wicked, especially in the Northern Kingdom of Israel. Few priests knew how to worship the true God. Elisha, God's prophet to Israel at this time, ministered in and around Mt. Carmel on the western edge of the Plain of Jezreel—a fruitful farming valley in northwest Israel. Shunem was a town in this valley, 18.5 miles away.

Getting to Know the Shunammite

Read 2 Kings 4:8-17.

Since this woman does not have a name other than "Shunammite," let us call her 'Shuna.'

What information is given about 'Shuna' (verse 8)?

What did 'Shuna' think about Elisha, and what did she suggest to her husband that they do for him (verses 9-10)?

How did Elisha respond to their generosity (verses 11-13)?

What need did she withhold (verse 14)?

Hearing about 'Shuna's' unexpressed need, what does Elisha, as God's representative, do about it (verses 15-17)?

'Shuna' and her husband gladly took care of Elisha's needs. They simply started with a meal, then turned their home into a "Bed and Breakfast" reserved for him whenever he was in town. This gracious gesture supported Elisha's ministry. Hospitality is a ministry. Women are particularly gifted by God to establish the warmth of a home—emotional and otherwise. Home is wherever you live and can serve as a great ministry tool.

Share a time when God has given you opportunity to use your home to minister to someone else.

About 5 or more years later...

Read 2 Kings 4:18-37.

What crisis was 'Shuna' facing (verses 18-20)?

How did she respond to the crisis (verses 21-22)?

Elisha represented God to her at this time. When 'Shuna' reached Elisha, what did she do and say (verses 27-28)?

How did Elisha respond to seeing her and to her words (verses 25-30)?

How was God faithful to 'Shuna,' and how did she respond?

A few years earlier, the prophet Elijah thought he was the only faithful God-worshiper left in Israel. God reassured Elijah that 7,000 people in Israel had not "bowed their knees" to Baal (1 Kings 19:14-18), being faithful to God alone. Perhaps Shuna and her husband came from those 7,000. Living in the midst of wicked Israel, this couple chose to remain faithful to God. God honored their faith by giving them opportunity to respond to His Word through Elisha whenever he came to their town.

At least 7 years later...

Read 2 Kings 8:1-6.

> *How did God show His faithfulness to 'Shuna' and her family (verses 1-2)?*

> *Now, what challenge was she facing (verse 3)?*

> *What did the king ask Gehazi to do (verse 4)?*

> *While Gehazi was speaking, what happened (verse 5)?*

> *How was God faithful to 'Shuna' again (verse 6)?*

Israelites could bypass lower officials and appeal directly to the king. Either someone had illegally occupied the woman's property, or it had fallen to the king's domain by virtue of its abandonment. Kings of Israel were not godly kings. Yet, God used this woman's faith story to move the king's heart to do what God wanted him to do.

Was 'Shuna's' sudden appearance before the king a coincidence? If not, what do you learn about our God?

After reading this passage, why do you think God allowed the family in Shunem to experience the crisis in 2 Kings 4?

What inspires you about 'Shuna'?

THE WALK FROM FEAR TO FAITH

What situations could have been fearful for 'Shuna'?

How did she respond to God by faith instead?

God loved 'Shuna' and her family. He knew what was going on in their lives. He was able to do something about it. But God did not make the woman's husband young again nor did God prevent her from enduring barrenness for a time. He did not prevent the famine from affecting their family. During her walk, a loving God said no to some things. Yet, she chose to trust Him rather than submit to fear. And He rewarded her faith with an outpouring of His blessing on her family. Likewise, God may not choose to fix your crisis so you experience no pain. But in any and all situations, you can count on these truths…

#1. God loves me
#2. God knows what is going on in my life
#3. God can do something about it
#4. I can trust His goodness in whatever He chooses to do

That is your walk from fear to faith.

JOURNAL YOUR FAITH STORY

God gave this woman a story of His faithfulness to her, and He gave her opportunity to share it with an ungodly king! Her faith led her to love God and His Word then led her to seek help from God in a time of pain and crisis. She learned to trust God.

Read Hebrews 4:14-16.

> *While there are times when family and friends can help us, God wants us to bring our deepest needs to Him alone. Describe a time you faced a crisis that only God could handle. Were you able to trust Him with the outcome? What happened? How was He faithful to you in this crisis?*

DECLARE GOD'S FAITHFULNESS

Recommended: *Listen to the podcast "Shunammite-Declare God's Faithfulness." Use the section below as a listener guide.*

Have you been in a really dark place with not even a glimmer of light?

When you are in total darkness, you look for light from any source, don't you? You see that light and follow it to get out of the darkness. That is what God does for us—He calls us out of darkness into His wonderful light. And He uses us as light-bearers to declare His faithfulness and lead other people to Him.

LIGHT-BEARERS DECLARE GOD'S FAITHFULNESS

We are God's dearly loved children who can be light-bearers to anyone still living in darkness.

> *But you are a chosen people, a royal priesthood, a holy nation, a people belonging to God, that you may declare the praises of him who called you out of darkness into his wonderful light. (1 Peter 2:9)*

You and I are chosen to be God's mouthpiece to the world around us. Our purpose is to declare what He has done in our own lives to those who cannot see the light. God's plan to meet that need for every woman is Himself through a relationship with His Son Jesus Christ.

JESUS IS THE LIGHT OF THE WORLD

Our God sent His Son Jesus into the world to lead the way out of the darkness. Jesus declared Himself to be the light of the world, giving sight to the spiritually blind (John 9). But He chooses to use us—frail, faltering, headstrong, often self-centered humans—to be his light-bearers and love messengers to the blind and fearful people we see!

We are the light-bearers. We communicate to those around us who are enshrouded in darkness that God is real and available to anyone who wants Him. That is the good news, "The Gospel."

THE GOSPEL — GOOD NEWS ABOUT GOD'S FAITHFULNESS

Christianity is Christ! It is all about a relationship with Him.

> Jesus Christ **laid down** His life **for** you so that he could **give** His life **to** you so that he could **live** His life **through** you. (Ian Thomas, *The Saving Life of Christ*)

If you have opportunity to tell someone one thing, tell her about Jesus.

➤ Tell her that God loves her and wants a relationship with her, but sin separates her from God's love.

➤ Tell her that Jesus is God, who came to earth as a man and died for her sins.

➤ Tell her that she can be completely forgiven of her sins and receive eternal life with God by believing in Jesus as her Savior.

DECLARE YOUR STORY OF GOD'S FAITHFULNESS

People love to hear stories. As you have learned to trust God's goodness in whatever is causing you fear, and journaled about it at the end of the lessons, you now have a story to share. Sharing your story is a simple way to speak about God's love for you and how He works in your life. You can bring hope to someone who needs it.

How did you first hear about Jesus? Someone told you, right? We get the awesome privilege of sharing that good news with others. There is such joy in reaching out to those who do not know Jesus and introducing them to Him so they can know Him just as you now know Him.

Think of it this way: Imagine you had cancer and were chosen to be part of a special test group for a new cure. The treatment cured all of your cancer completely free of charge. What is the first thing you would do after you were healed? You would blast it all over Facebook, telling all of the other cancer victims about this great cure! Well, sin is a cancer affecting every single person. And you have been cured—forgiven of your sins—by your faith in Jesus Christ.

Do you remember how you felt before you believed in Jesus? Maybe you felt lonely, guilty, and without hope. Maybe you were afraid. You have a story to share about your walk from fear to faith. Your story illustrates the power of God in your life, His faithfulness to you that helps you let go of your fear and trust His goodness. You do not need to be an expert in the Bible or have years of experience knowing Christ. Just share what you know.

And as you declare God's faithfulness to you on your walk from fear to faith, be sure to include the four truths you have learned that are essential to faith:

#1. God loves me
#2. God knows what is going on in my life
#3. God can do something about it
#4. I can trust His goodness in whatever He chooses to do

God will continue to show His faithfulness to you as you walk from fear to faith.

REFLECT

God gave this woman a story of His faithfulness to her, and He gave her opportunity to share it with an ungodly king! God has given you a story to tell of His faithfulness to you. Review the various parts of your story that you have already written in the lessons. Choose one or two to expand into your story to share of your faith walk with God, especially your WALK FROM FEAR TO FAITH. Write it out below. Think in terms of what you can share in about 5 minutes. Then ask God to give you opportunities to share your story!

"My Walk from Fear to Faith"

For a more detailed study of these and other Old Testament women, check out the *Everyday Women, Ever Faithful God* study on melanienewton.com.

Apply Faith To Fear

The information below is a great tool to use whenever you are afraid. It will lead you to apply faith to your fear.

1. **Confront** it. What fears do you have right now? Think about them. The worst ones, the real ones, and the imaginary ones.

2. **Ask** about each one: What is my worst-case scenario? Consider just one of those fears. What is the worst that could happen? Think realistically.

3. **Consider**: If the worst I can imagine happens, could I handle it through the presence and power of Jesus Christ? As a believer, you have the power of the One who created the Universe living inside of you. Can He help me get through anything? Remember Romans 8:26—the Spirit Himself is praying for you in your weakness when you don't even know what to ask for.

4. **Remember** these four truths:

   #1 God loves me. *John 16:27; Romans 5:5, Ephesians 5:1*
   #2 God knows what is going on in my life. *Matthew 6:31-32; Psalm 139:1-10*
   #3 God can do something about it. *Genesis 18:14; Luke 1:37; Mark 10:27*
   #4 I can trust His goodness in whatever He chooses to do. *Psalm 119:68; Proverbs 3:5*

5. **Pray**: Prayer is simply talking to God about anything and everything.

   - Thank the Lord for His presence and His goodness.
   - Ask Him for the courage and peace to ride out the storm. Where the Bible is clear, you can claim God's promises by faith.
   - Anytime, you can ask for deliverance and protection—but you cannot hold God to promises He has not made. He has not promised immunity from natural calamities, illness, and troubles.

6. **Live life** securely in Him:

   - Take common sense precautions. Be wise in the world.
   - Trust God to show you what to do and give you strength when you are weak.

Sources

The following resources were used in the preparation and writing of this study.

1. A.T. Robertson, *Robertson's Word Pictures of the New Testament,* Broadman Press, 1932.

2. Bryant Wood, "The Walls of Jericho," *Creation* magazine, March 1999.

3. David Meece, "Things You Never Gave Me" lyrics

4. MercyMe, "Bring the Rain" lyrics

5. John F. Walvoord and Roy B. Zuck, *The Bible Knowledge Commentary Old Testament*, Victor Books, 1985.

6. Shannon Wexelberg, "In the Waiting" lyrics

7. The NIV Study Bible New International Version, Zondervan Bible Publishers, 1985.

8. Victor Hamilton, *Handbook on the Pentateuch*, page 91

9. Ian Thomas, *The Saving Life of Christ*

10. Lauren Daigle, "Trust in You" lyrics

11. Mike Messerli quote (accessed at searchquotes.com/mjmesserli)

www.ingramcontent.com/pod-product-compliance
Lightning Source LLC
Chambersburg PA
CBHW070807120626
46557CB00002B/743